THE ULTIMATE YOUTH CHOIR BOOK

COMPILED AND EDITED BY ROBERT STERLING

Arranged by Robert Sterling

with Steven V. Taylor, Dennis Allen and Gary Rhodes

D1379444

THE ULTIMATE YOUTH CHOIR Book

COMPILED AND EDITED BY ROBERT STERLING

Arranged by Robert Sterling
with Steven V. Taylor, Dennis Allen and Gary Rhodes

COMPANION MATERIALS

Choral Book	301 0350 015
Cassette	701 9811 507
Double Compact Disc	701 9811 590
Cassette Trax (Split)*	301 4353 086
Double CD Trax (Split)*	301 9811 589

*"Split-Trax" format (left channel, instrumental;
right channel, vocals minus solos)

Music Engravings by
BILL WOLAVER, BRYCE INMAN & DANNY ZALOUDIK
Piano Transcriptions by
BILL WOLAVER & BRYCE INMAN
Project Editor:
BRUCE COKEROFT
Cover Design:
DEWALL, POLLEI & COWLEY

 This symbol indicates a track number on the accompaniment Compact Disc. Selecting a given CD track number will start the accompaniment track at the corresponding musical section indicated in the choral book.

WORD MUSIC

CONTENTS

FOREWORD

This tremendous volume of music and resource materials
for youth may well be one of the most useful ministry tools
to come along in many years. Robert Sterling has compiled
twenty of the most popular songs for youth and combined
them with practical, useable dramas, a musical, a Worship
Service for youth, congregation and reader's theater. In
addition, fresh, new devotionals which correspond to each
of the songs have been included. The song order in the
music portion of the book and on the recorded product
remains consistent with the order of performance in the
dramas, musical and Worship Service. The strength of the
chosen arrangers on this collection speaks for itself. We are
truly excited about the practicality and versatility of this
project and are confident that you will agree!

WORD MUSIC

Field of Souls

Words and Music by
WAYNE WATSON
Arranged by Gary Rhodes

Performance Time 5:38

but, dif-f'renc-es a-side,

we will work the field of souls,

to-geth-er you and I.

3rd time to CODA

12

and   who has   la - bored best? ___
in   si - lence   on ___ her   knees, ___

Oh, that   life de - vot - ed   to ___ our   God, ___
___ be - fore the throne ___ day   af - ter   day, ___

That   life   de - vot - ed   to ___
Be - fore   the throne ___ day   af -

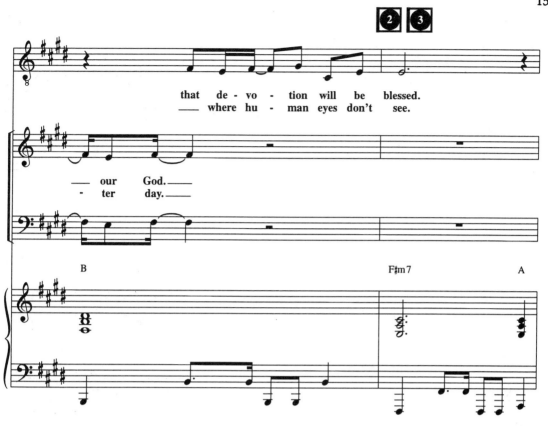

Oh, to - geth - er.

We work the field of souls,

to - geth - er you — and I.

58

We work the field — of souls,

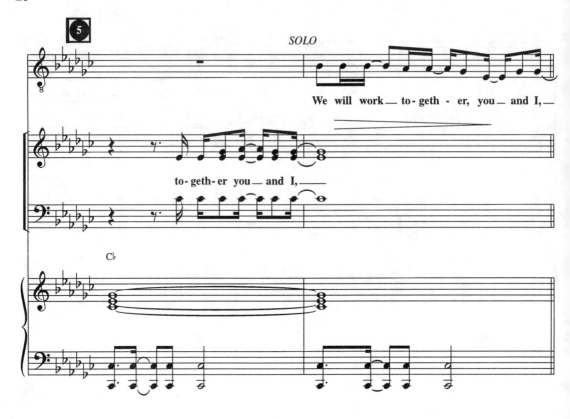

We will work — to- geth - er, you — and I, —

to- geth- er you — and I, —

C♭

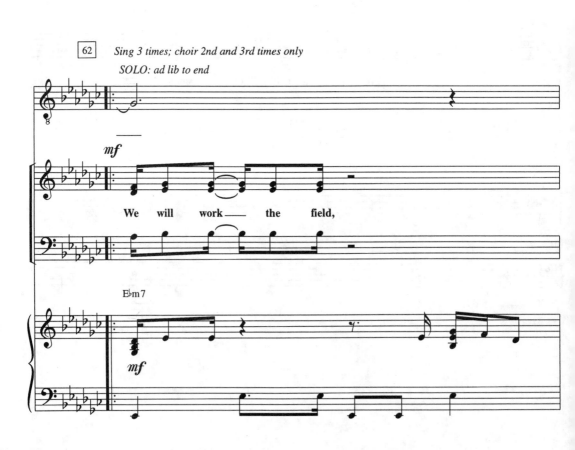

62 *Sing 3 times; choir 2nd and 3rd times only*

SOLO: ad lib to end

mf

We will work — the field,

E♭m7

mf

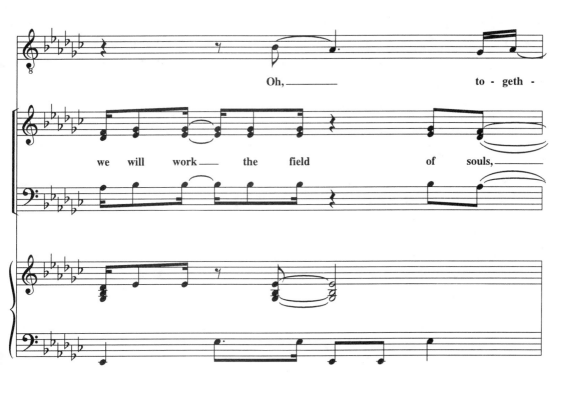

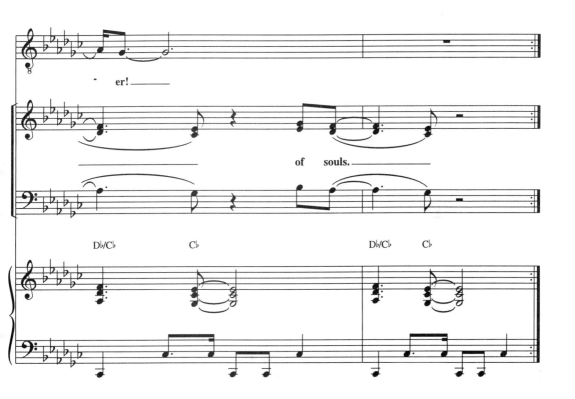

More Than Anything

JON MOHR and
RANDALL DENNIS
Arranged by Robert Sterling

1st time: SA unis. mel.
2nd time: CHOIR

God loves peo - ple more — than an - y - thing, —

Performance Time 3:35

God loves peo-ple more—— than an-y-thing.——

Fm7   Eb/F   Bb   Eb

14

Ab/Eb   Bb/Eb   Eb
SOLO: with some freedom

1. God loves the wea-ry—— when
2. God loves the wound-ed—— who've

mp

Ab/Eb

they're too weak—— to try.—— He
stum-bled in-to sin.—— He

feels   their   pain,____   He   knows____   their   shame;____   He and
reach - es   down____   and   pulls____   them   out____

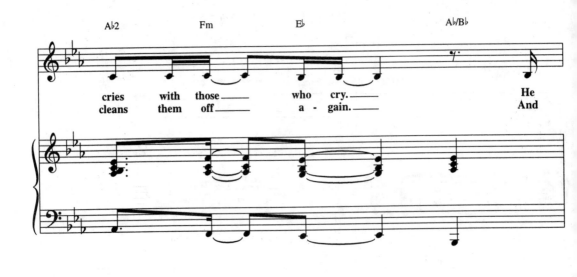

cries   with   those____   who   cry.____   He
cleans   them   off____   a - gain.____   And

18

won't   give   up____   or   walk____   a - way____   when
He   will   heal____   the   bro - ken____   heart____   that's

Dying to Reach You

Words and Music by
GEOFF THURMAN
and MICHAEL PURYEAR
Arranged by Steven V. Taylor

Performance Time 4:11

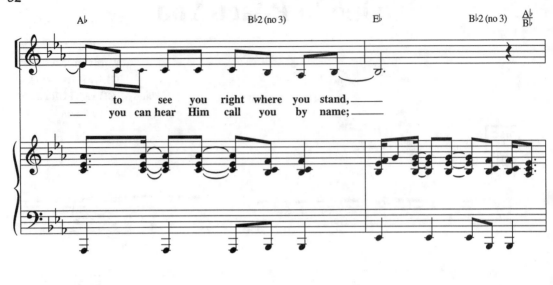

to see you right where you stand,
you can hear Him call you by name;

He emp - tied all of Him - self
He sim - ply wants to for - give

so He could reach out His hand
all of the guilt and the shame.

o - pen___ your heart ___ 'cause He's dy - ing___ to reach___ you.

to reach you,___ dy - ing___ to reach___ you.___

A♭   B♭2 (no 3)   E♭   B♭2 (no 3)   A♭/B♭

A♭   B♭2 (no 3)   E♭   B♭2 (no 3) A♭   Fm7(4)

I Will Tell the World

Words and Music by
RAY BOLTZ
Arranged by Dennis Allen

Performance Time 3:41

ev - 'ry - one___ to know.___
make my voice___ your own.___

C   D

25 *f*

I will tell the___ world He

25 G   C   D

is re-turn - ing. I have touched the___

G   C   Cmaj7/E

46

48

49

50

Go Light Your World

Words and Music by
CHRIS RICE
Arranged by Gary Rhodes

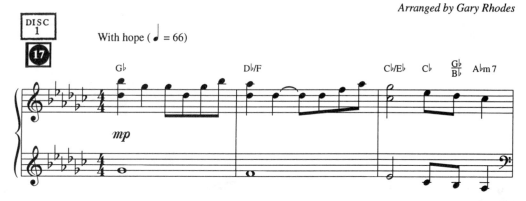

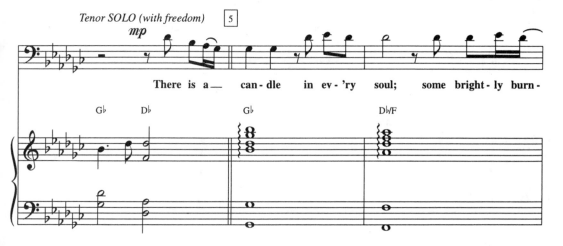

Performance Time 4:20

56

60

61

Jesus Will Still Be There

ROBERT STERLING

JOHN MANDEVILLE
Arranged by Robert Sterling

Performance Time 4:29

I'll Lead You Home

Words and Music by
MICHAEL W. SMITH
and WAYNE KIRKPATRICK
Arranged by Steven V. Taylor

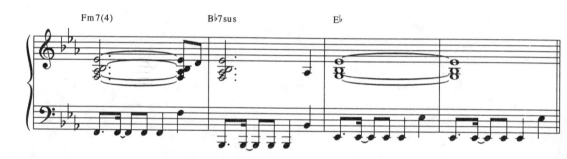

1. Wan - der - ing — the road of des - p'rate life —
2. A trou - bled mind — and a doubt - er's heart, —

Performance Time 4:51

Just Reach Out

Words and Music by
JOHN SCHLITT and RICH GOOTEE
Arranged by Robert Sterling

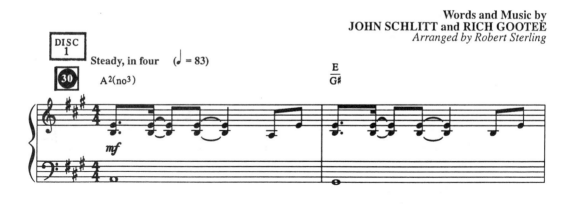

Performance Time 3:10

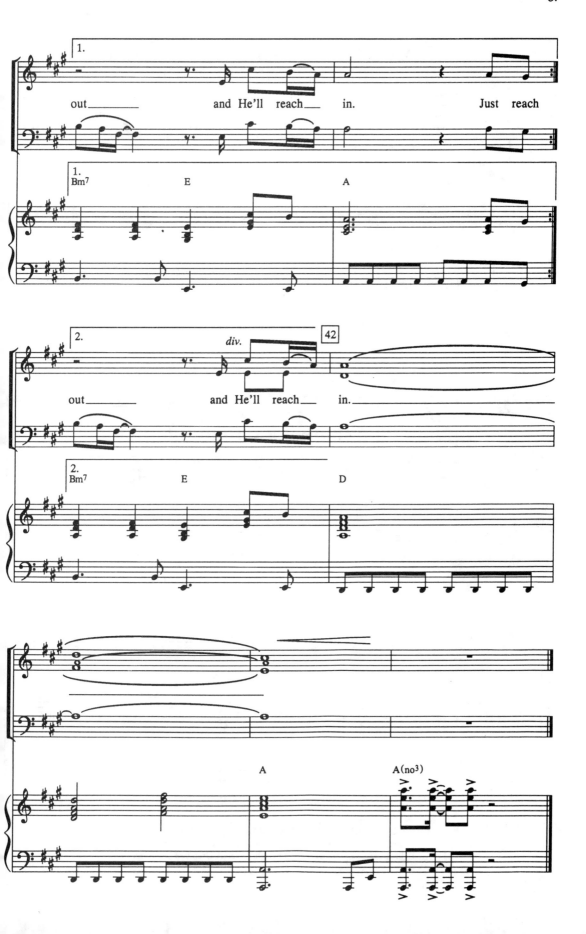

Heaven Is Counting on You

Words and Music by
RAY BOLTZ and STEVE MILLIKAN
Arranged by Robert Sterling

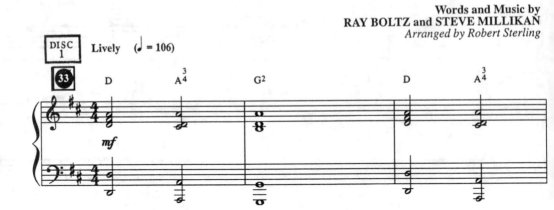

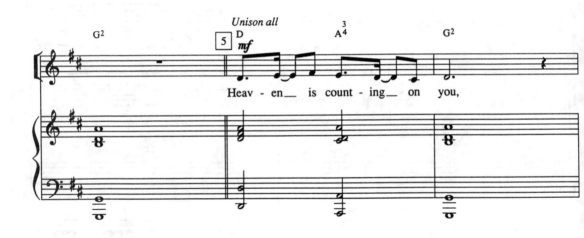

Performance Time 3:18

94

Look What God Is Doing

Words and Music by
SCOTT WESLEY BROWN,
DWIGHT LILES and NILES BOROP
Arranged by Steven V. Taylor

Performance Time 3:04

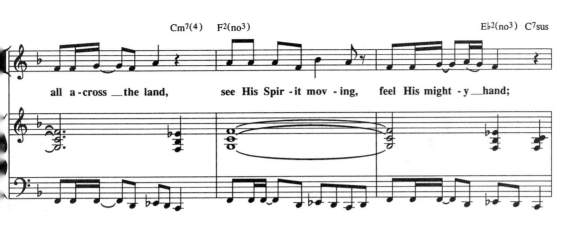

all a-cross __ the land,   see His Spir-it mov-ing,   feel His might-y __ hand;

break-ing chains of dark - ness,   set-ting cap-tives free,

look what God is do - ing through those __ who do be-lieve. __

17 *mf*

Glo - ry hal - le - lu - jah! __ Look _____ what God is

melody

F   Dm⁷ Gm/C Dm⁷ Gm/F   F   Dm⁷ Gm/C Dm⁷

21 *SOLO: Both times*

do - ing! ____   He is call - ing faith - ful men __ to
                 Take the liv - ing gos - pel, _____

mp

Gm/F   F   Gm⁷   F²/A

SOLO: Both times

car - ry out __ His plan, __ so   in the pow'r __ of Je - sus' __ name
mix it with __ some love, _____   add a lit - tle act - ion _____ and

B♭   Csus   C   Gm⁷   F²/A

100

Hallowed Be Thy Name

Words and Music by
BABBIE MASON and ROBERT LAWSON
Choral Arrangement by Steven V. Taylor

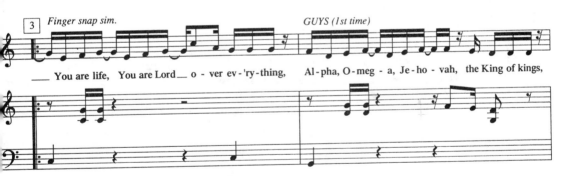

Performance Time 2:57

ALL

Won-der-ful, Way__mak-er, wor-thy of my of-fer-ing; hal-low-ed be Thy__name.__ You are love,__

2.

SOLO

hal-low-ed be Thy__name.__ You're the an - swer to all__ of my prob-lems and you solve them

9

ALL SOLO

Hal-low-ed be Thy name.__ You sup-ply____ all my needs__ and I call__ You Ab-ba Fa-ther__

C G G/B F C

Hal-low-ed be Thy __ name. __   Hal-low-ed be Thy __ name. __

Hal-low-ed be Thy __ name. __   Hal-low-ed be Thy __ name. __

Hal-low-ed be Thy __ name. __   Hal-low-ed be Thy name.

You Are Holy

CAROLYN ARENDS
and MARK HARRIS

MICHAEL W. SMITH
Arranged by Robert Sterling

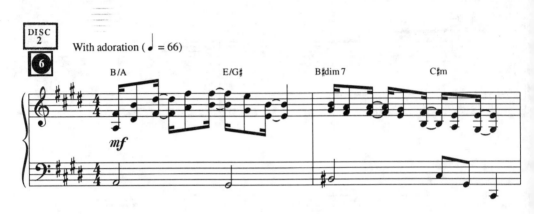

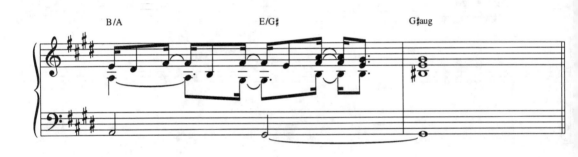

1. Here   be - fore Your   throne   I've come to
2. When   Your love breaks through   and I am

Performance Time 4:10

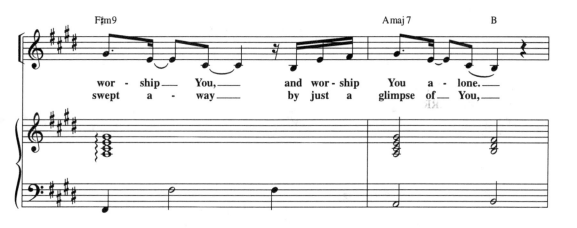

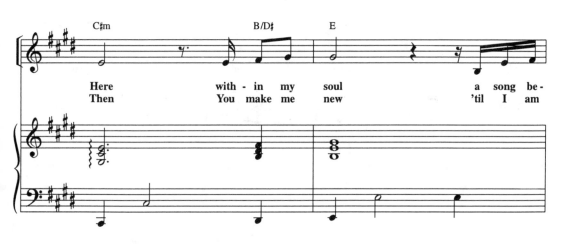

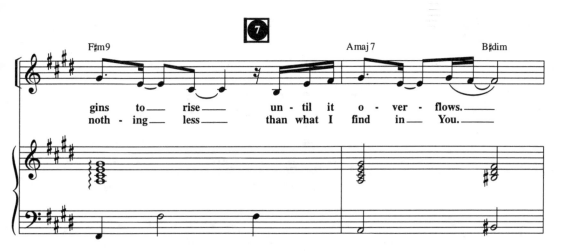

114

Lord.

Lord.

Un-to the One who sits on the throne, and un-to the Lamb, be all

bless-ing and hon-or and glo-ry and pow-er and praise. Woh,—

Un - to the One who sits on the throne, and un - to the Lamb, be all

bless- ing and hon- or and glo- ry and pow- er and praise.

All cre - a - tion

and in heav - en and earth we make known:

sings,

Shine on Us

Words and Music by
MICHAEL W. SMITH
and DEBORAH D. SMITH
Choral arr. by Gary Rhodes

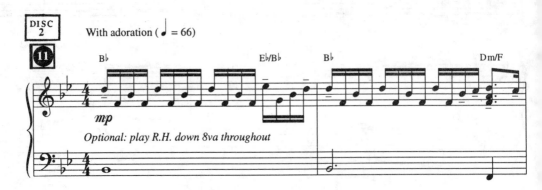

Performance Time 4:01

123

124

The Love of Christ

**WES KING and
MICHAEL CARD**

**WES KING and
MICHAEL W. SMITH**
Arranged by Robert Sterling

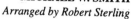

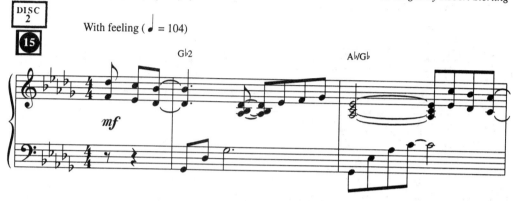

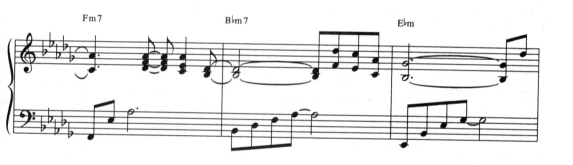

Performance Time 3:48

128

130

132

134

deep is the love _____ of Christ. _____

Ab7

Db7 sus/Cb

20

Gb2/Bb

56

Ooo _____

E no 3rd

B/D#

A

I Must Tell Jesus

Words and Music by
Rev. E. A. HOFFMAN
Arranged by John Andrew Schreiner
and Brian Tankersley
Choral Arrangement by Gary Rhodes

2. I must tell

148

108

mf unis.

Je - sus can help me,____

Je - sus a - lone.

decresc.

mp

p *

decresc.

p

* *Track fades quickly after choral cutoff.*

Love One Another

Words and Music by
MICHAEL W. SMITH
and WAYNE KIRKPATRICK
Arranged by Robert Sterling

* GUYS: opt. 8va (falsetto unis. with Girls)

Performance Time 4:49

lu - tion to my world's___ de - mise."___ He said the
walked the earth, but I nev - er found___ _ an - y

jour - ney would be long, but this___ is where___ you start.
cor - ner of the world___ where this___ did not___ ap - ply.

CHOIR

Love one an - oth - er,___ love one an - oth -

know with-out a doubt you can change your world with love.

GIRLS TRIO

And look-ing out__ I saw__ no meth-od to__ the mad-ness there,__

CHOIR

If the peo - ple of the land___ u - nit - ed, then I be-

lieve we'd all___ a - gree___ that we should start a - gain___ and this.

would be___ our creed: Love one an - oth - er, ___ er, ___

'cause you know with-out a doubt, you can

unis.

change your world with love.

(Begin opt. ad lib to ms. 80)

1.

Love one an-oth- change your world.

div.

2. 32

Ooo_____ Ooo Ooo_____

F/G   C/G

Ooo Ooo_____   You can

Am7(b5)   G/B   A/C#

1.

change your world with love._____

1.
Eb/F   G

(* GUYS: opt. 8va unis. falsetto with Girls)

Lover of My Soul

AMY GRANT

MICHAEL OMARTIAN
Arranged by Steven V. Taylor

Performance Time 4:18

17 F2   G   Am

And then the sun comes up   slow-ly with the dawn,

F2   G   F/G   C

this is   the kind of feel-ing   that I   hang my hope up-on.   There is a love

F2/A   G/B   C   C/E   F

and beau-ty   in   all   that   I   see,

Eb   Bb/D   **34** Gm   F/G   F/C   C

and no one, no - bod-y   is ex - plain-ing You to me.

things that I know, _____

Dm7(4)   C

29

ten - der   and sweet   and

F2 (no 3)

strong   as   my ___ need; _____

Dm7(4)   C

give me faith___ to ful - ly be - lieve___ that the

D.S. al CODA

end SOLO

Mak- er of ___ this whole wide ___ world is a Fa- ther to ___ me!" ___

CODA

47

I need the voice, ___ I need the touch. ___

CODA

53

a tempo

And may - be my eyes can't see,____

F2 (no 3)

but You are sur - round - ing me.

Dm7(4)   C

38

Here in the wind and rain____ the

F2 (no 3)

174

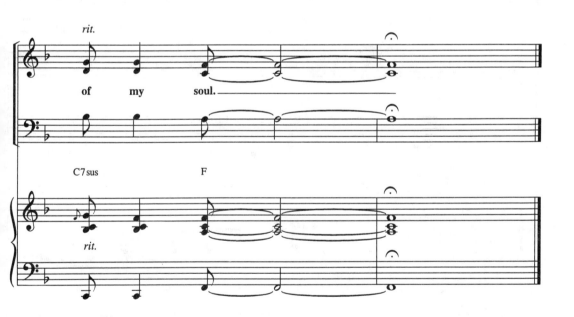

The Rock
(That Was Rolled Away)

TERRY COX

ARNIE ROMAN, ERIC BIBB
and TERRY COX
Arranged by Steven V. Taylor

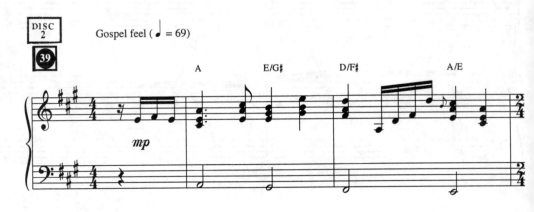

Performance Time 4:07

trou - bles all a - round;____ My de -
strength to bear the load;____ Give me

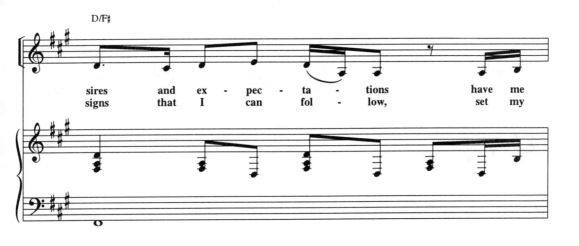

sires and ex - pec - ta - tions have me
signs that I can fol - low, set my

lost more than I'm found.____ And Lord
feet up on the road.____ And may

Breath of Heaven
(Mary's Song)

Words and Music by
CHRIS EATON
and AMY GRANT
Arranged by Robert Sterling

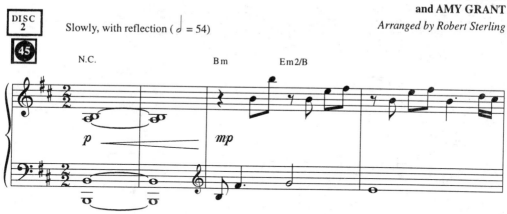

Performance Time 5:16

oth - er ___ one   should have

if an - oth - er, ___

Bm   Em/B   G2

had   my ___ place? ___   But I of - fer ___

mf   78

Ah ___

Bm   A   D   E2sus   Em

mf

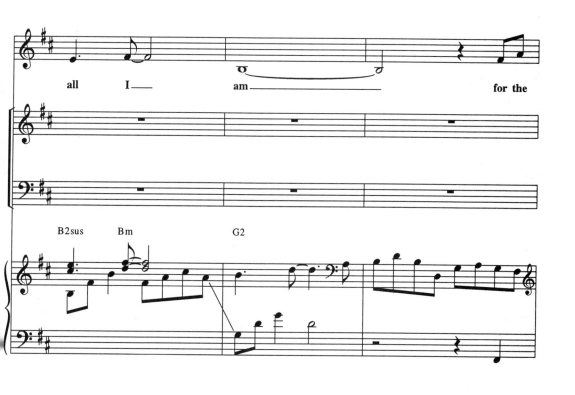

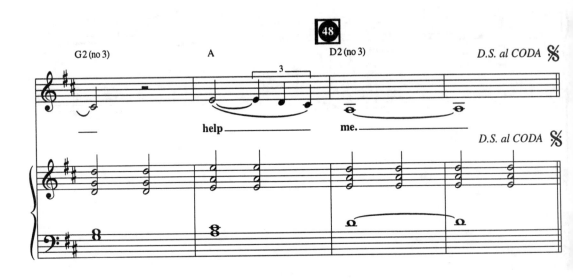

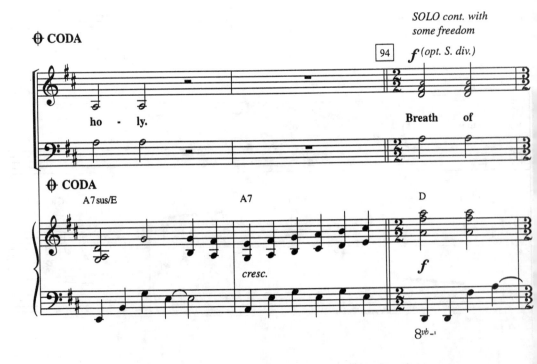

198

Spread the Word

Words and Music by
KARLA WORLEY and
ROBERT STERLING
Arranged by Robert Sterling

Performance Time 2:13

Order Form
Youth Choir

The Ultimate Youth Choir Book

___ Choral Book	$ 6.95	301 0350 015	___
___ Cassette	15.95	701 9811 507	___
___ CD	19.98	701 9811 590	___
___ ACC (split)	80.00	301 4353 086	___
___ ACD (split)	90.00	301 9811 589	___

****

HOW TO ORDER

☎ BY PHONE
Call Toll Free 1-800-933-9673, ext. 2037 (M-8:00-5:00 CST).

Please have all order information available when calling.

Unless faster service is specified, all orders will be shipped via UPS.

✉ BY MAIL
Complete the order form at your convenience, be sure to specify quantities on the lines provided.

Total your order (shipping & handling will be added).

Fill out the address information below.

Mail to: **Word Music Resources**
P.O. Box 2518
Waco, TX 76702-2518

Processing will begin the day your order is received. We will bill your account.

QUANTITY DISCOUNTS AVAILABLE!*

10% Discount

15% Discount

10-19 Quantity   20+ Quantity

*Discounts do not apply to trax, orchestrations and other companion products.

☐Church Address   ☐Home Address

(Please Print)

CHURCH _____

MY NAME _____

STREET/P.O. BOX _____

CITY/STATE/ZIP _____

CHURCH PHONE ( ) _____ HOME PHONE ( ) _____

phone number must appear for confirmation.

Priority Code 03640

The Latest Word

for Youth Choir

Winter 1995

The Ultimate Youth Choir Book

Compiled & Edited by Robert Sterling
Arranged by Robert Sterling with Steven V. Taylor,
Dennis Allen, & Gary Rhodes

New from Word Music comes this wealth of material for youth choir. *The Ultimate Youth Choir Book* is an outstanding compilation of easy-to-sing arrangements that will make any youth choir sound great and feel successful. There are twenty songs, along with dramas and devotionals creating a multi-purpose resource book for youth choirs.

You'll find songs here from popular Christian artists like Point of Grace, Amy Grant, Clay Crosse, 4HIM, Michael W. Smith and others. The songs were selected because of their meaningful message, including evangelism, commitment, devotion, and praise and worship.

The drama scripts offer great variety in this collection. You can create up to a 45-minute musical with one, while another offers a twenty-minute musical option.

What an excellent ministry tool for your youth choir. Great songs and hot tracks make this non-seasonal collection <u>the</u> perfect choice for any youth choir.

For all your Word Music needs, call Toll Free

1-800-933-9673 ext. 2037

The Ultimate Youth Choir Book
Devotionals by C. Gene Wilkes

"Field of Souls"
. . . we will work the field of souls, together you and I . . .
(song begins on page 9)

If you are from a farming community, you know how important harvest time is. You have only a matter of days to get the crop out of the field before it rots or weather destroys it. You don't sleep or go on vacation when the crop is ready to harvest. Sometimes you hire extra help to make sure the goods get in before winter.

When Jesus saw all the people following Him, He had compassion on them. He saw they were helpless and in need. He turned to his disciple and asked them to pray to the "Lord of the harvest" to send workers into the fields ready for harvest. The field of souls was ready for harvest, but there were not enough workers. You live in a field of souls. Will you sleep through the harvest or go to work?

"The harvest is plentiful but the workers are few." Matthew 9:37

Next Step: Your friends are like a field of souls ready for harvest. Who do you know that you can go to and share the message of Christ? Who can you take with you? Plan a project with friends to go into your field and join God in harvesting souls.

"More Than Anything"
. . . God loves people more than anything . . .
(song begins on page 23)

God loves people more than anything. Right. More than anything? Show me. Okay, look at Jesus. God sent His only Son in the form of a person. He could have been an angel, creature or spirit, but God sent Him as a person so He could save people. He was a person just like you and me; same body functions, drives and hungers. (He just never broke God's rules with them.) In Jesus, God showed us what God looks like in a person. God wanted us to touch, feel, taste, see and hear what a relationship with God was like. Jesus: God in person sent to save real people.

Here's the punch line: God allowed people to kill His Son on a cross so they could have eternal life! Now, you tell me—if God let people kill Jesus so His death would allow those same people who trusted Him go to Heaven, doesn't that show God loves people more than anything? I think so.

"But God demonstrates His own love for us in this: While we were still sinners, Christ died for us." Romans 5:8

Next Step: Take a moment to ponder the awesome price God paid to show you how much He loves you. Show Him your appreciation. Show His love to someone else.

"Dying to Reach You"
. . . you are one of the ones that He was dying to save . . .
(song begins on page 31)

Did you hear about Mickey Mantle's new liver? Someone had to die so he could live a little longer. He eventually died of cancer, but God used his funeral to tell millions about Jesus. The donor in heart and liver transplants must die so a sick person can live.

That's what Jesus did. He died so you could live. You were sick in sin, destined to spend forever separated from God. Jesus took on your sickness, died and donated eternal life to you. The difference between Jesus and other donors is that He is alive to enjoy your new life with you!

"And He died for all. . . " 2 Corinthians 5:15

Next Step: Make a short list of everything you have done today that would tell a doctor you are sick with sin. You know: selfish acts, rude words, lustful thoughts. Offer this list to Christ in a prayer and thank Him for dying so you could live.

"I Will Tell the World"
. . . here I am, send me, I will go . . .
(song begins on page 43)

Isaiah went to church one day, and God showed up! He was a priest doing His priestly routine, when angels, smoke and God Himself filled the temple. Isaiah confessed he was not fit to be in the same room, but God forgave him and cleaned him up. When God asked who He could send to tell the world about His love, Isaiah volunteered.

God may not send angels to your church service, but, in Christ, God has forgiven you and cleaned you up. God is looking for people to send and tell the world of His love. How can you say no?

"Here am I. Send me!" Isaiah 6:8

Next Step: What has God called you to do? Make a list of things you can do today that God has asked you to do. Remember, every long trip begins with the first step.

"Go Light Your World"
. . . carry your candle, run to the darkness . . .
(song begins on page 53)

Ever have the lights go out in your house? Pretty dark, huh? You stumble around until you find a candle and a match. Sometimes you can find a flashlight that works. Everyone is relieved when light pierces the darkness. You can't hide light. You can see Amarillo in the Texas Panhandle twenty miles before you get there because of the lights.

Jesus said His followers are the light of the world. Jesus also said that you don't put a candle under a bowl. You put it on a stand so everyone in the house can benefit from it. You have the light of Christ in your life. Now, run to the darkness. Someone needs the light.

"You are the light of the world." Matthew 5:14

Next Step: Turn out the lights in the room. Sit in the darkness. What do you feel and hear? Now, light a match or turn on a flashlight. Feel better? That's how people who are living in darkness feel when you show them the light of Jesus.

"Jesus Will Still Be There"
. . . When it looks like you've lost it all and you haven't got a prayer . . .
(song begins on page 62)

Do you remember the story of Daniel? He trusted God, but ended up at the bottom of a pit with hungry lions sniffing his arms and legs. Rival politicians had fooled the king into making a law that would remove Daniel from their career paths to the top. They knew Daniel would never stop praying to his God. That's how they trapped him. Daniel was on his way out.

By most standards, Daniel didn't have a prayer. Indiana Jones would have trouble getting out of this one. Daniel had to wonder if God had blessed him only to become Cat Chow for so many mangy lions. The going got real tough, but Daniel never wavered from his faith in God. In the night, God sent an angel to stand with him. The lions never got supper. That same God sent Jesus to be with you. What pit are you in? Jesus will still be there . . .

"My God sent His angel, and he shut the mouths of the lions. They have not hurt me." Daniel 6:22

Next Step: Draw a picture of the pit you see yourself in. Name the lions sniffing at your feet. All alone, ask God to send His Spirit in that pit to protect you. Trust God to love you and stand in the pit with you.

"I'll Lead You Home"
. . . When you are lost and alone . . .
(song begins on page 70)

Have you ever looked up and realized you were lost? No landmarks. No friendly places. Most people do this when they are children. Did you ever wander away from Mom while she was squeezing oranges in produce, and you ended up all alone in another aisle, or worse? Tears stop when mother and child get together again. When you are lost, relief is spelled F-O-U-N-D. You get lost by willfully or unintentionally leaving the path. You get found when someone who cares comes looking for you.

Jesus told a story about a shepherd who owned 100 sheep. One got lost, so the shepherd went to look for it. He found it and brought it home. When he got home, he threw a big party and invited his friends over to celebrate with him. Jesus says we are like lost sheep. The Good News is that Jesus is the Good Shepherd who is out looking for us. Lost? Listen. Hear Him calling?

". . . the sheep listen to His voice. He calls His own sheep by name and leads them out." John 10:3

Next Step: Share with the group when you were the most lost, how you felt and who found you. Look around this week for someone who is lost. Lead them to Jesus.

"Just Reach Out"
. . . it doesn't matter who you are or where you've been . . .
(song begins on page 81)

You remember Zacchaeus: the short, rich guy nobody liked? He did not set out to get elected to be the loneliest, least-liked Jew in Jericho. He needed work, and collecting taxes for the Romans from his neighbors seemed like a great idea at the time. But the more he stole from them and the more people he hurt, the more his heart hardened and the easier it was to hunker down with his bank roll. Zach knew what it meant to stand in a crowd and still be all alone.

Zach reached out to Jesus one day by climbing in a tree to see over the crowd. Jesus reached into Zach's life by going home with him for dinner. In the end, Jesus made Zach's broken heart whole again because the "sinner" reached out to Jesus. He can change your heart, too. Just reach out. It doesn't matter who you are or where you've been.

"Jesus said to him, 'Today salvation has come to this house, . . .'" Luke 19:9

Next Step: Put yourself in Zach's short body. What is going on in your life that has made you climb a tree to reach out to Jesus? Share it with your choir director or close friend. Jesus will reach in to help if you will ask.

"Heaven Is Counting on You"
. . . and the saints beyond cheer us on today . . .
(song begins on page 88)

If you have ever run a race in a stadium filled with people, you know the thrill of crowds cheering for you. If you have never run a race like that, maybe you have sat in a stadium and cheered your favorite athlete or team. Cheering from supporters helps you run faster and play harder.

The writer to the Hebrews encouraged his readers by reminding them that "a great cloud of witnesses" surrounded them. Imagine that. While you are down here running the race of life, Christians before you are cheering you on. That's right. Christians like Paul, Peter, Lydia and Phoebe. Your Christian aunt or grandfather are there, too. They are cheering for you because they are counting on you. Wanna race?

"Therefore, since we are surrounded by such a great cloud of witnesses . . . let us run with perseverance the race marked out for us." Hebrews 12:1

Next Step: Write a list of Christians who you know are in heaven cheering for you. What are they cheering for? How does this make you feel?

"Look What God Is Doing"
. . . see His Spirit moving . . .
(song begins on page 96)

Missouri is the "Show Me" state. They live by the old saying, "Seeing is believing." Their patron saint is Doubting Thomas. Remember Thomas? He asked for proof of the resurrection directly from the guy who was there. When it comes to faith, most of us are from Missouri.

John the Baptist sent his disciples to ask if Jesus was really the Sent One of God. Some time had passed since John baptized Jesus, and his followers were wondering when they were to change unions. When John's followers asked Jesus if He was for real, He told them to "Look what God is doing." The blind received sight, the lame walked, and the good news was preached to the poor! "Proof is in the pudding!" Jesus was the Sent One. Just look around.

"Go back and report to John what you have seen and heard . . ." Luke 7:22

Next Step: What does it take to convince you God is real and at work around you? Miracles? Healings? Jesus said trusting was more valuable than seeing. Try trusting without seeing for a week. Your faith will grow.

"Hallowed Be Thy Name"
. . . Wonderful Waymaker, worthy of my offering . . .
(song begins on page 103)

<u>Hallowed</u> is an older way of saying holy. Holy means set apart, different, like no other. Holy is who God is. God is holy because there is no other being like Him. Holy means God is Lord over everything. Also, to call one's name is to call the person. Try inviting someone to be a friend without knowing her name.

In prayer, to call God's name is to call the person of God. "Our Father," calls to the Father who is in heaven. When Jesus taught His disciples to pray, He made sure they admitted that God was holy by telling them to pray "hallowed be Thy name." God is holy. Different. Not someone you casually ring up for a chat. Respect and honor belongs to God.

"This, then, is how you should pray: Our Father in heaven, hallowed be Your name." Matthew 6:9

Next Step: Who is the most respected person in your life? How do you approach him? How do you talk to her? Compare your answers with how you talk to God. Stand and repeat prayerfully the Lord's Prayer.

"You Are Holy"
. . . We will offer You our praise in a mighty chorus . . .
(song begins on page 110)

Praise is simply telling someone what you like about them. Praise honors the person by stating something special about them. When you praise God, you honor Him by saying or singing something unique about Him. When you praise God by singing, "You are Holy," you honor Him by saying, "You are untouchable, unreachable and perfect in every way." You also say, "I am nothing like You."

Praising God is what angels do. God created some of them to do just that. Others are special agents of God. Others protect people for God's purposes. In heaven, angels gather around the throne of God and praise Him for all time. Someday you will join them on the other side. Better to start practicing now . . .

"To Him who sits on the throne and to the Lamb, be praise and honor and glory and power for ever and ever." Revelation 5:13

Next Step: Get alone. Be quiet. Imagine yourself before the throne of God surrounded by angels. Quietly repeat Revelation 5:13 several times. Then sing the words from the song. This is praise. Try this with your choir at practice, too.

"Shine on Us"
. . . that we may have life to find our way in the darkest night . . .
(song begins on page 118)

What's the first thing you ask someone who walks up to you in a dark place? You ask, "Who is it?" Right? You also look for some light on the person's face to know if he is a friend or not. Light helps you recognize people.

The Bible says: "God made His light to shine on our hearts." He did this "to give us the light of the knowledge of the glory of God in the face of Christ." God shined His light in our hearts so we could recognize Jesus, so we could recognize the face of God in the night. That's what this song is about.

"For God . . . made His light shine in our hearts . . ." 2 Corinthians 4:6

Next Step: Try to read your music in a poorly lit room. Turn up the lights little by little until you can see it clearly. Now you can see the words. Now you can understand. Pause as a choir and ask God to shine His light on you so you can know what you are singing.

"The Love of Christ"
. . . how wide, how long, how high, and how deep is the love of Christ . . .
(song begins on page 127)

Have you ever stood on the edge of the Grand Canyon? Did you know that its total length is 217 miles? It is more than one mile deep in places and ranges from four to eight miles wide! Plateaus on either end of the canyon rise 5,000 to 9,000 feet above sea level. Now that's some canyon! If you have ever seen this natural wonder, you probably cannot imagine anything to compare with it.

When Paul prayed that the Christians in Ephesus would know how wide, long, high and deep is the love of Christ, he had never seen the Grand Canyon. He didn't need to. He had experienced something far greater in Christ's love when God forgave him for persecuting the church and chose him to go to the world with the Good News about Jesus.

"And I pray that you . . . may have power, . . . to grasp how wide and long and high and deep is the love of Christ." Ephesians 3:17, 18

Next Step: What is the largest thing you can think of? Christ's love for you is greater. Stop and ask God to show you how massive His love for you is.

"I Must Tell Jesus"
. . . He is a kind, compassionate friend . . .
(song begins on page 139)

You tell secrets to friends. The best time is late at night after everyone else is asleep and the two of you start telling each other what you are really like. You spill your guts about how you feel about your parents and what people say about you at school. You finally admit you like the Homecoming Queen, and you both laugh until you cry. You tell how God seems more real than ever. You pray God would fix all the broken stuff in your life. You feel compelled to tell everything to your best friend. Four in the morning rolls around, and you finally go to sleep.

Jesus is that kind of friend. You can tell Him all of your troubles and how your heart is tempted to sin. He is the late-night best friend you can go to when you must tell someone your deepest, darkest hurts and secrets. He can help you when no one else will even listen. Go tell Jesus. He loves and cares for His own.

"You are my friends if you do what I command." John 15:14

Next Step: Take a minute and imagine Jesus is in the same room with you. You trust Him with all your heart. What would you tell Jesus since He <u>is</u> here?

"Love One Another"
. . . just a fundamental law that we should all live by . . .
(song begins on page 152)

Have you heard stories of a friend who swam out to save his friend, and they both drowned? Lifeguards would say the friend got too close to the one in trouble. That's true in life saving. Not so in friendship. Friends risk everything to be together when danger is near.

Jesus said we are to love one another just as He loved us. He said there is no greater love than to lay down your life for your friends. He knows. That's what He did for you. Look at the cross . . .

"My command is this: Love each other as I have loved you." John 15:12

Next Step: Someone in your group is hard to love. You may never know why they are that way, but Jesus said to love them anyway. What can you do today that can change their world with love?

"Lover of My Soul"
. . . the Maker of the whole wide world is a Father to me . . .
(song begins on page 163)

Everyone wants to be loved. Actually, that is how God made you. You do your best stuff when you know someone loves you. People who don't know they are loved spend their whole lives looking for it. You want to hear "I love you" from a parent, friend—even God, more than anything else in the world.

When God says, "I love you," He does something to show it. His greatest expression of love is sending His only Son to die in your place so you get God's love rather than God's wrath. God, the Creator of the universe, loves you . . . all the way down to your soul. What more do you need to hear?

"For God so loved the world, that He gave His one and only Son that whoever believes in Him shall not perish but have eternal life." John 3:16

Next Step: Have you ever told anyone you loved them? If so, what did you mean when you said it? Remember, to love like God always includes action with the card and candy. Now, have you ever done something to tell someone you loved them?

"The Rock (That Was Rolled Away)"
. . . let the Rock that was rolled away be my cornerstone . . .
(song begins on page 176)

The rock that was rolled away from the tomb symbolizes the risen Christ. Do you know what that means? Paul said that if Jesus was not raised from the dead, then you should be pitied most of all people. If God did not roll away the stone at Easter, you are trusting in a fairy tale. An empty tomb is the foundation of faith.

A cornerstone determines the strength and squareness of a foundation. If your cornerstone is wrong, the whole building will fall down. You must have something sure to build your life upon. The risen Lord who sits at the right hand of the Father and who will return to judge all people is the best thing to have under your house. Until you are in His presence, let Him be your cornerstone.

"I lay a stone in Zion, a chosen and precious cornerstone, and the one who trusts in Him will never be put to shame." 1 Peter 2:6

Next Step: Tour your downtown. Look for buildings with visible cornerstones. If your life was a building, what have you built it upon? If you have a cornerstone that you can depend upon to keep things standing and safe, what is it? Jesus can be your cornerstone if you don't have one.

"Breath of Heaven"
. . . I offer all I am, for the mercy of Your plan . . .
(song begins on page 187)

Mary. Unmarried, pregnant teenager. How do you tell that to your parents? How do you tell that to your fiancee–with whom you have never had sex! How do you tell your best friend who knows you are a virgin. They'll all swear you are lying; especially when you tell them an angel said you would become pregnant when "the Holy Spirit will come upon you, and the power of the Most High will overshadow you." Them?! How do you convince yourself this is happening?

Mary had two choices. Cut out for the nearest bus station, or, stay and trust God in all this. Mary stayed. Joseph believed, and Mary began to show at three months. God chose Mary because she trusted Him. God knew this quiet, faithful teenager would offer herself to do God's perfect plan for the world–even if it didn't make sense at the time. How about you? What would you do?

"I am the Lord's servant," Mary answered. "May it be to me as you have said." Luke 1:38

Next Step: Has God ever asked you to do something that seemed impossible to you? What was it? Now, put yourself in either Mary or Joseph's sandals. You think if God could do that, surely God could do what He's asked you to do?!

"Spread the Word"
. . . once you've heard, you've got to spread the word . . .
(song begins on page 199)

When was the last time you heard some juicy information? Somebody likes somebody else. So and so failed his English exam. If you've got the goods on someone, you have a hard time keeping it to yourself. Good news is like that, too. Someone has a new baby sister, or your best friend found out she is getting a new car for Christmas. Once you've heard, you've got to tell someone else.

The shepherds who watched their sheep outside Bethlehem 2,000 years ago couldn't keep the news to themselves, either. Angels—an army of them—woke them from their sleep to tell them God's Sent One was born in the town near their flocks. When they found the baby Jesus lying in a feeding trough just like the angels said, they told as many people as they could before they returned to keeping sheep. They had to tell someone. Wonder if they slept much the next night?

"When they had seen Him, they spread the word concerning what had been told them about this Child." Luke 2:17

Next Step: What has God shown you from the Bible, in prayer or in conversation with a friend? Go to a friend and tell her what you learned about Jesus.

Brief Bio of C. Gene Wilkes

Gene served as a youth minister for fourteen years in the local church. He spent two years as Executive Director of a private foundation, specializing in youth camps and conferences. He has been the pastor of Legacy Drive Baptist Church in Plano, Texas, since April of 1987. He and his wife, Kim (whom he met at Baylor University, Waco, Texas), have two daughters, Summer, a fourth grader, and Storey, who is in the seventh grade. Somewhere in all that he earned a Ph.D. in New Testament from Southwestern Baptist Theological Seminary, Fort Worth, Texas. Gene's hobbies are writing and golf.

The Ultimate Youth Choir Book
Drama Resources
Written/Compiled by Keith Ferguson

he drama resources that follow are provided to enhance some of the songs in
iis collection. They are flexible and easy to use, enabling the director to piece
gether two or more songs for a concert setting, individual selections for
orship, or complete musical/dramatic programs.

here are six sketches that fit together with individual songs:

ONG	SKETCH
esus Will Still Be There"	"Lost and Found" by Shaun Walvoord
'll Lead You Home"	"Midnight Guilt" by Randy Kilpatrick (from DRAMA FOR YOUTH, Vol. 1 Product #3010010486)
Ieaven Is Counting on You"	"Heaven Can't Wait" by Keith Ferguson (from DRAMA FOR WORSHIP, Vol. 8 Product #3010011482)
Must Tell Jesus"	"Honest to God" by Rich Peterson (from DRAMA FOR WORSHIP, Vol. 3 Product #301000348X)
over of My Soul"	"What a Friend?" by Holly Baber (from DRAMA FOR YOUTH, Vol. 2 Product #3010014481)
Breath of Heaven"	"MARY/Mary" by Holly Baber

*u'll notice that most of the sketches above are from Word Drama's DRAMA FOR
OUTH or DRAMA FOR WORSHIP series. These are also excellent resources for your
uth Choir program, so check them out! You may find several sketches to do with
usic, or, as "stand-alone" dramatic pieces.*

In addition to the individual scenes above, there are two Musical Drama "packages" or programs. One is a brief Musical on evangelism entitled **"FIELD OF SOULS,"** using 5 songs. There are 6 characters in the musical. The other program is a **Worship Service** entitled **"SHINE ON US,"** using 4 songs. It uses a Reader's Theater style of narration and Scripture readings. There are 4 readers. (They don't even have to memorize the material—just read effectively!)

"FIELD OF SOULS"—MUSICAL—Theme: Evangelism
by Keith Ferguson

SONGS:
"Field of Souls"

"More Than Anything"

"Dying to Reach You"

"I Will Tell the World"

"Go Light Your World"

"SHINE ON US "—WORSHIP SERVICE WITH NARRATORS/READERS
by Keith Ferguson

SONGS:
"Hallowed Be Thy Name"

"You Are Holy"

"Shine on Us"

"The Love of Christ"

LOST AND FOUND
by Shaun Walvoord

CAST
Clerk (Male or Female)
3 Teenagers (Male or Female)

SET/PROPS
The clerk could be standing behind a counter or a service window with a "Lost and Found" sign hung above it.

(as the scene begins, the 3 teenagers enter the "Lost and Found")

Clerk:	Welcome to "Lost and Found." How may I help you?
#1:	Well, I've lost something and I was wondering if it has been—well, if it has been . . . found?
#2:	Yeah! *(gesturing to self and #3)* Us, too!
Clerk:	Then you have certainly come to the right place. Specifically, what are you and your friends looking for?
#1:	Well, I've misplaced my wallet.
#3:	I think I left my school backpack somewhere.
#2:	And I seem to have lost . . .
Clerk:	*(interrupting)* Hold on now—wait a minute. I'm afraid I must stop you there.
#2:	How come?
#1:	Yeah. What's the matter? You said this place was the "Lost and Found"—right?
Clerk:	That's true. But it's not that kind of "Lost and Found."
#3:	Really? Then what kind is it?

Clerk:	I guess the best way to explain it is like this: The things the three of you have lost are temporary possessions—things that will not last anyway, even if you found them. Here, at "Lost and Found" we find things that are more . . . well . . . more lasting.
#1:	More lasting?
Clerk:	Here. I'll show you what I mean. Tell me something you have lost. Something <u>BIG</u>. Something <u>really</u> hard to find.
#1:	Well . . . (*thinking*) There is one thing—but I don't see how you could possibly find . . .
Clerk:	(*interrupting again*) Go ahead. Give it a try.
#2:	(*to #1—in a stage whisper*) Might as well. There's nothing to lose.
#1:	Okay. It's like this: All of my life I've moved around a lot because of my Dad's job. As soon as I get close to people, I have to move away.
Clerk:	And what have you lost from all this moving around?
#1:	I guess I've lost my ability to reach out to other people. I've lost my ability to trust. I'm not proud of that. It's just how it is.
Clerk:	(*pondering*) Lost your ability to trust. Let me help you find it. (*looks through pages in Bible*) Aha! Here it is. According to my Boss, you can know one that is "closer than a brother." Not only that, but H (*looks through more pages*) "will never leave you or forsake you."
#1:	(*thinking about it*) You know, wouldn't it be great if your Boss is right?
Clerk:	Oh, He is—believe me.
#1	Really? (*smiles*) Thanks mister! (*or ma'am*)
Clerk:	(*to #2*) And what about you? What have you lost?
#2:	For me it's the fact that my parents have been talking about getti a divorce. I know that happens all the time. Some people would say, "It's no big deal." But it is to me! These are the only parents I've got. Now, they are always fighting and screaming and stuff! It's like, my whole life is up in the air.

Clerk:	I see.
#2:	I've been so worried about it that I can't sleep at night.
Clerk:	So, you have lost your sense of peace.
#2:	Yeah. That's it.
Clerk:	Good news! Here's how to find it: (*opens Bible and reads*) "Come unto Me, you who labor and are heavy laden and I will give you rest."
#2:	For real?
Clerk:	For real.
#2:	Your Boss says that, too?
Clerk:	Sure thing! It's right here. (*shows him the Bible*)
#2:	That's amazing!
#3:	(*excitedly*) Hey! My turn! It's my turn next!
Clerk:	What have you lost?
#3:	Hmmm. Oh, I dunno.
Clerk:	Try me.
#3:	I guess you could say, I've lost my hope.
Clerk:	Why?
#3:	Sometimes, it just seems like there's really not a point to living. I seem to move one step forward and two steps back. I just feel like I'm losing ground. Life is just so rough, sometimes, that's all I'm saying. I find myself asking, "Is this really all there is to life?" "Is there any hope of things getting better, any hope at all?"
Clerk:	This is where you find it. (*opens Bible again and reads*) "God has chosen to make known the glorious riches of this mystery, which is Christ in you, the <u>hope</u> of Glory."
3:	You mean your Boss can guarantee that I can find this hope?

Clerk:	Absolutely!
#2:	Hey! I was wondering something. What is that book you keep getting all this stuff from?
Clerk:	It's the Bible.
#2:	The Bible . . . I've heard of that.
Clerk:	Yep. It's where all the lost get found.
#2:	So this isn't some "fly-by-night" operation, huh? I mean, your Bos has been doing this for a while?
Clerk:	Oh, it seems like an eternity. And He'll always be here for you. He not going anywhere—that's for sure.

(*music begins*)

"JESUS WILL STILL BE THERE"

MIDNIGHT GUILT
by Randy Kilpatrick

CHARACTERS

EDDIE-	16-19
SAMANTHA-	16-19
STORMY-	16-19
PRESTON-	16-19
LANDON-	16-19
REBECCA-	16-19

SETTING/PROPS
An empty stage. Depending on the style you choose, the actors could dress uniformly in all black, or dress in a style appropriate to their characters.

(*Three actors [victims] are obscured behind three other actors. Before the victims speak they will come from behind the other actors. At the end of their segment, they will retu to their original positions.*)

EDDIE: I don't guess I'll ever forget that night. How could I? I re-live it over and over again in my dreams. There are nights I wake up in a cold sweat and I can see the intersection and the light changing. I can hear the laughter from the back seat. I can even feel my foot press harder on the accelerator—we're going to make it . . . we will . . . just a little faster . . . just another second and we'll be through.

(*pause*) And that's where the nightmare ends . . . a split-second of excruciating pain and then—blackness.

(*SAMANTHA moves up from behind him, turns and faces the audience*)

SAMANTHA: "Just another party," you said. "Why don't we all ride together," you said. "I'll drive," you said. (*pause*) At least you survived. That's more than I can say for me.

EDDIE: I know! I live with it every day!

SAMANTHA: I died with it. (*longer pause*) How many drinks? Four . . . ten?

EDDIE: I don't remember. If it's any consolation, I can't even taste a beer now without thinking about . . . you.

SAMANTHA: And I can't even think about you . . . you took that privilege from me. Who would I have become?

EDDIE: I don't know.

SAMANTHA: Who would I have loved?

EDDIE: I don't know. But . . . I loved you . . . I loved you.

(*SAMANTHA returns to stand behind EDDIE, as STORMY moves into position*)

STORMY: You said that if I loved you . . . really loved you . . . I would prove it.

RESTON: But I didn't know.

STORMY: You said that I was the only one . . . your <u>only</u> one.

RESTON: I lied to you . . . I needed you that night.

STORMY:	Like you "needed" all the others?
PRESTON:	But I didn't know.
STORMY:	How many "others" are there? How many others have you killed?
PRESTON:	(no response, shakes head)
STORMY:	How long have you had it? How long have you known?
PRESTON:	I didn't know . . . I didn't. I didn't think it could happen to me . . . not to us. I'm healthy, I'm not sick. AIDS is somebody else's disease, not ours. We're too young. We have our whole lives ahead of us.
STORMY:	Not anymore . . . not anymore.

(STORMY returns to her place behind PRESTON and LANDON moves to his place)

LANDON:	I don't even have a name. I don't really know if anyone knows me. In heaven, the angels have a name for me. I think it means . . . "The Unwanted One." My mother, if you can call her that, decided . . .
REBECCA:	(interrupting) What do you mean, "if you can call her that." I'm still your . . . mother. I still love you. I still think about you.
LANDON:	If you loved me . . . why didn't you want me to live?
REBECCA:	I don't know. I was so young. It was a long time ago. But . . . I think about you every day. You haunt my nights. When I see children playing . . . I wonder. I wonder what you'd look like. I wonder if you would be as happy as they are. I wonder . . .
LANDON:	Me, too.

(LANDON returns to his place behind REBECCA. The music begins for "I'll Lead You Home." As this is sung, a JESUS character could move among the characters, embracing them, and leading them offstage; leading them "home.")

"I'LL LEAD YOU HOME"

HONEST TO GOD
by Rich Peterson

CHARACTERS

LU -   eager to learn

ELAINE -   eager to teach, uses a stereo-typical "Brooklyn" accent

SETTING/PROPS

This scene can be effectively performed on a blank stage with no props.
However, the use of props may enhance some segments of the scene.

LU: My prayer life seems to be taking a turn for the worse. I don't
             have the desire to pray like I used to have.

ELAINE: Have you tried the Lord's prayer? That always works for me.

LU: What? Just pray through the Lord's prayer?

ELAINE: No. Elaborate on it, embellish it, really get into each part of the
             Lord's prayer. You oughta try it, Lu, I'm tellin' ya. It works.

LU: I'll try it. (*ELAINE turns her back*) Our Father, which art in
             heaven, hallowed be Thy name. Thank you, Lord, that You are
             Jehovah Tsidkenu (*SID-KAV-NEW*), my righteousness. Elaine!

ELAINE: Yeah, Lu.

LU: I tried it. For the last six months I've been praying through the
             Lord's prayer, and . . .

ELAINE: And?

LU: And it's been great, really great, but now my prayer life seems to
             be taking a turn for the worse. I don't have the desire to
             pray like I used to have.

ELAINE: Have you tried location praying?

LU: Whatzat?

ELAINE: You know—at the river today, the park tomorrow—you know,
             location praying.

LU: Oh—you mean vacation praying.

ELAINE: Whaaat?

LU: Mini-vacations with God.

ELAINE: You got it. Get off alone with God—seek His face—new
           environment—maybe you'll hear Him better—who knows?

LU: I'll try it! (*ELAINE turns her back*) Our Father, which art in
           Heaven, thank You for this catfish pond I'm praying beside. May
           the fish within experience joy today in knowing You care for
           them . . . as fish. (*hits a mosquito on her arm*) Elaine!

ELAINE: What! What!

LU: It isn't working!

ELAINE: What—so you don't like location praying?

LU: It worked. For the last six months I've prayed in every location
           except the great wall of China and it's been great—but do you
           know what?

ELAINE: What, Lu?

LU: My prayer life seems to be taking a turn for the worse. I don't
           have the desire to pray like I used to have.

ELAINE: Have you tried position praying?

LU: (*skeptical*) Whaaatt—?

ELAINE: Yeah. Change positions when you pray. Stand, sit, lie on your
           face, walk around, kneel—you know, break up the monotony.
           Keep your body guessing and your tongue intercessing! That's
           my motto!

LU: I'll try it! (*ELAINE turns away*) Dear Lord, I kneel before You
           now (*she does*) as I stand (*stands*) in Your presence . . . falling on
           my face (*she does*) in reverence to Your power and (*walks and
           stomps*) treading down serpents and principalities and leaping
           (*leaps*) as a deer on Your mountain of spices as I rest (*lies
           down face up*) before You. I'm rolling (*somersaults forward*)
           all my burdens on You and falling (*she falls*) in love with You m
           each day. (*lies, then still*) Puff . . . puff . . . puff . . . I die daily . . .
           lying as dead men . . . my sins . . . wiped out . . . and me . . .

puff . . . puff . . . a heavy offering . . . unable to rise in Your presence . . . Puff . . . puff . . . puff.

ELAINE: *(turning to her)* Lu? You alright?

LU: Could you help me up?

ELAINE: What were you doing?

LU: A combination of position, location and prayer aerobics.

ELAINE: Looks more like dislocation aerobics.

LU: Can't complain. I've lost fourteen pounds in prayer since Tuesday.

ELAINE: Wow, that's great—but how's intercession goin'?

LU: Well, my prayer life seems to be taking a turn for the worse. I don't have the desire to pray like I used to have.

ELAINE: Well, I've got one last trick—and this one always works for me. Team prayer.

LU: Sounds good. How does it work?

ELAINE: You get a bud—like me—and we pray together.

LU: Oh? Is that like group prayer?

ELAINE: No—it's different—it's the prayer of agreement. Whatever you pray, I echo in agreement with you.

LU: That does sound good.

ELAINE: Wanna try it? We can try it right now if you wanna.

LU: Oh, how do we start?

ELAINE: You start and I'll follow in behind you.

LU: Here goes . . .

(As LU prays, ELAINE echoes every word, starting at LU's third word. ELAINE speaks simultaneously and loudly—a bit obnoxiously even! LU doesn't stop between sentences.)

LU: Dear Lord—be with Mrs. Jenkins at the pharmacy
ELAINE: Dear Lord—be with Mrs. Jenkins at

LU: today . . . and help Mr. Jenkins at the garage . . . I thank You
EL the Pharmacy today . . . and help Mr. Jenkins at the garage. . .

LU: for ELAINE who is helping me learn to team pray with her,
EL thank You for myself, who is helping Lu learn to pray

LU: *(slows down with big pauses in between words)* and—for—
EL with myself, *(slows down and speeds up with what LU does)*

LU: friends - who - will - give - time - to- *(very fast)* teach
EL and - for - friends - who - will - give - time - to -

LU: everything they know about prayer and intercession so
EL teach *(fast)* everything they know about prayer and

LU: they can become the prayer warriors they want to be!
EL intercession so they can become the prayer warriors they want
be!

(LU stops and looks at ELAINE with exasperation. ELAINE slowly smiles back as if to say, "Isn't this just great?" The next prayer increases in volume and speed as it goes.)

LU: I pray You will help me to resolutely be resolute to
EL *(pause)* I pray You will help us to resolutely be

LU: resolve our resolutely resolve to be resolutely resolved
EL resolute to resolve our resolutely resolve to be

LU: resolutely. Let our resolute resolve be resolute that we
EL resolutely resolved resolutely. Let our resolute resolve

LU: might resolutely resolve our resolute resolves resolutely
EL be resolute that we might resolutely resolve our resolute

LU: to resolutely resolve our resolute resolutes resolutely
EL resolves resolutely to resolutely resolve our resolute

LU:	being resolute to resolve. . . (*grows to a shout*) THIS IS
EL	resolutes resolutely being resolute to resolve (*grows to a shout*)

LU:	NOT WORKING!!!!!!
EL	THIS IS NOT WORKING!!!!!!!

ELAINE: What's the matter, Lu? You seem . . . tense.

LU: I don't know, Elaine. All these plans and guidelines are great, but I don't seem to be able to consistently touch the heart of God.

ELAINE: Don't tell me—your prayer life seems to be taking a turn for the worse, and you don't have the desire to pray like you used to have.

LU: BINGO.

ELAINE: Well, the Bible does say something about this, you know.

LU: It does? Where?

ELAINE: Romans 8:26. "Likewise the Holy Spirit also helps our weaknesses; for we don't know what to pray for as we ought to, but the Holy Spirit Himself intercedes through us with groanings too deep for words according to the will of God."

LU: So maybe I should ask the Holy Spirit to help me? I've asked everyone else.

ELAINE: It couldn't hurt. Just be honest. Tell Him you've been having problems praying to Him. Ask Him for help. Formulas are great and they get you a framework to work from, but ya gotta get beyond the outline and really commune with Him. Tell Him the way you really feel . . . but don't yell at Him. Tell Him in a nice way . . . He is holy, you know. And Lu, you've told me. You can tell Him—He's been listenin' to ya anyway. Besides, if you can't be honest to God, who can you be honest to? See ya.

(*she turns away*)

(*music begins*)

"I MUST TELL JESUS"

WHAT A FRIEND?
by Holly A. Baber

CHARACTERS

WISDOM-	either gender
HUMILITY-	either gender
SENSITIVITY-	either gender
KASEY-	girl, 15-18

SETTING/PROPS
None required

(as the scene opens, KASEY is seated center and appears rather bored)

KASEY: OK, so what if it's another Friday night and I have nothing to do. So what if everyone else is out doing stuff. Have any of them called me? No. Who needs them?

(WISDOM enters)

WISDOM: Can I help you?

KASEY: I hope so. Who are you?

WISDOM: *(shakes head)* Oh boy, it's worse than we imagined. I am Wisdom.

KASEY: Really? Are you a rapper?

WISDOM: *(to audience)* This isn't going to be easy. *(facing KASEY)* We're here to help you out. You need work in the friendship area.

KASEY: I'm a good friend.

WISDOM: You're OK. You need to add more of us to your lifestyle. Let's begin with wisdom. I am very important to the friendship process.

KASEY: I'm pretty smart already.

WISDOM: "How blessed is the man who finds wisdom, and the man who gains understanding."

KASEY: What?

WISDOM:	If you have wisdom, you also have the gift of understanding. These are two of the ingredients of being a friend.
KASEY:	What are the others?
WISDOM:	Humility and Sensitivity. These are gifts from the Holy Spirit. (*leans over and speaks confidentially to KASEY*) You don't have many friends for us. The people you know are only acquaintances.
KASEY:	So?
WISDOM:	So getting closer to God will help you find us some friends. I am dying for stimulating conversation. Have you ever tried to talk to your other emotions? It's not easy.
KASEY:	Why are you telling me this?
WISDOM:	You need to go to God and ask Him to re-teach you to be friendly. We'll never win souls at this rate. (*exits*)
KASEY:	I don't need "Friend Therapy"! I do just fine alone.
	(*HUMILITY enters*)
KASEY:	Who are you?
HUMILITY:	I didn't think you'd recognize me. Look at me. I'm all dusty. (*blows dust off arm at KASEY*)
KASEY:	(*coughs*) Great. What do you want?
HUMILITY:	I want you to listen.
KASEY:	To what?
HUMILITY:	To God. The Lord will let the humble sit with the princes of His people.
KASEY:	I don't want to sit with princes!
HUMILITY:	But you want to win souls for God, don't you? Have you forgotten the Great Commission? A sour Christian is one of the crowning works of the devil.
	(*HUMILITY exits and stands by WISDOM*)

KASEY:	What do you mean, "sour." I'm not sour! (*yells*) I'm an extremely pleasant person!

(*SENSITIVITY enters and taps KASEY on the shoulder*)

KASEY:	Who are you?
SENSITIVITY:	I'm your Sensitivity. You and I are going to close our eyes and hold hands and try to tap into your soft side . . . I'm sur it's in there . . . somewhere.
KASEY:	Oh no, we're not!!
SENSITIVITY:	To spread God's love, you need to learn to tame your huma need to do everything your own way. You need to be gentle and listen with a tender ear and . . .
KASEY:	You're talking like a girl.
SENSITIVITY:	I am not a girl—I'm an emotion. I'm a feeling, sensitive par of your make-up that you've conveniently neglected. (*Hits KASEY on the arm*) I'm not the only thing you've neglected. You've neglected God.
KASEY:	That's ridiculous.
SENSITIVITY:	You've been so busy with yourself that you've lost all of your communication skills. We don't talk to anyone! Not even God. You're messing up! (*pause*) God is the best frienc you can give yourself. And, when you have Him you'll war to be friends with others.
KASEY:	Why don't you crawl back inside my brain or wherever it i you came from?
SENSITIVITY:	The Spirit has been speaking to us. Why won't you let us answer?
KASEY:	I haven't heard anything.
SENSITIVITY:	(*begins to look frightened*) Of course you've heard it. It's so loud we haven't been able to concentrate. It sounds like yo grandmother's voice. It's singing a song from your childhood. It's always your favorite hymn. (*pause*) You dor remember it, do you? (*SENSITIVITY sadly walks over to WISDOM and HUMILITY*) I tried.

WISDOM:	You did your best.
HUMILITY:	I guess we'd better go back.
KASEY:	(*trying to remember some of the words*) What a friend we have in Jesus . . . (*HOLY SPIRIT enters and steps forward and speaks*)
HOLY SPIRIT:	I was hoping you'd recognize me. It has been long time, but . . .
KASEY:	. . . all our sins and briefs . . . no . . . all our sins and griefs to bear . . . wait a minute . . . is that right?
HOLY SPIRIT:	I feel like we don't talk anymore. I know you're busy, but so am I, you know?
KASEY:	. . . what a privilege to carry everything to God in prayer.
HOLY SPIRIT:	(*crosses in front of KASEY to stand on the other side*) What I'm saying is I make time for you, but you won't make time for me. I can tell you're lonely, but you aren't letting me help.
KASEY:	. . . oh, what peace we often forfeit . . .
HOLY SPIRIT:	You stop by church occasionally, but you're only there to make an appearance. I remember when you couldn't wait to talk to me. We did everything together. Now, I'm not a part of your life. I'm just an after-thought . . .
KASEY:	. . . oh, what needless pain we bear . . . all because . . .
HOLY SPIRIT:	I've tried to talk to you many times, but you brush me off.
KASEY:	. . . all because . . . uhmm . . . all because . . .
HOLY SPIRIT:	But now that I've got this opportunity, there is something I've been trying to say . . .
KASEY:	(*stops singing*) I can't believe I've forgotten that song. Oh, well. It'll come to me eventually. (*exits, crossing in front of the HOLY SPIRIT*)
HOLY SPIRIT:	(*watches KASEY leave, pauses, and quietly says*) I wanted to tell you that I love you . . . and I miss you very much.

(lights fade to black as the music begins)

"LOVER OF MY SOUL"

HEAVEN CAN'T WAIT
by Keith Ferguson

CHARACTERS

JACOB–   a heavenly citizen
MIKE–   another heavenly citizen

SETTING/PROPS

The scene is a street in Heaven. However, there are no visual clues to the location in the set or the costumes. As far as the audience is concerned, it could be anywhere, until they begin to listen to the conversation between the characters. A park bench for the characters to sit on would be a nice touch.

(as the lights fade up, we see two guys, JACOB and MIKE, walking toward each other)

JACOB: Hey Mike! How's it goin'? I haven't seen you in weeks. What have you been up to?

MIKE: Oh, not too much. Same old stuff . . . worship . . . choir practice . . . little more worship . . . harp lessons . . . back to worship again . . . you know. What about you?

JACOB: Well, I've really gotten into the recreational end of things. On Mondays I go to Paul's Tent Making Class, on Tuesdays it's Boat Building with Noah and then on Fridays it's my favorite: surfing lessons with Peter.

MIKE: Wow!

JACOB: It's cool, man! He doesn't even use a surf-board!

MIKE: You're kidding!

JACOB: Nope. He said we should be able to do it soon. Anyway, next week I'm taking the "Water into Wine" seminar, and "Dancing with David."

MIKE: That's great. They'd <u>never</u> let us do any of that in my part of town.

JACOB: Where's that?

MIKE: Baptist Land. All we do is eat and go to committee meetings.

JACOB: Bummer.

MIKE: Hey, don't knock it. The fried chicken is heavenly.

JACOB: Very funny. Let's sit down and visit for awhile. You got time?

MIKE: Nothing but.

JACOB: How long have you been here?

MIKE: Let's see . . . that's a tough one. It's kind of hard to keep track of time up here. But . . . I'd say it's been at least a couple of years.

JACOB: Is all of your family here yet?

MIKE: Oh, no. That's a pretty scary thought, too. A lot of my people back home are . . . uh . . . well . . . not headed in the right direction.

JACOB: Mine too. I've got lots of family and friends down there I'm praying for. Don't you sometimes wish you could go down, just for a few minutes, and talk to them?

MIKE: I know! It's wonderful here . . . but I'm so afraid they're never going to find Christ. For instance . . . look over there. That's my brother, Mark. He thinks he's OK because he's a good guy. You know, he's faithful to his wife . . . loves his kids . . . pays his taxes, and goes to church every now and then. But . . . he doesn't know Jesus. And then, over there . . . my old friend Derek. He's very smart and successful . . . drives a Mercedes . . . but, he's a fool.

JACOB: What do you mean?

MIKE: He doesn't believe in God and God said, "Only the fool says in his heart that there is no God." If we could just get them a message . . .

JACOB: But we can't. It's up to them. (*points downward, "peering over the edge"*) The church.

MIKE: Yep. (*looking at the earth, "below"*) You think they'll ever get serious?

JACOB: They better. Time's gettin' short. Seems like Gabriel's been practicing an awful lot lately.

MIKE: Yep. He sounds like he's ready to go, too. (*looks down again*) Now, see that group over there . . . they're feeding all those hungry people. That's great! But . . . it's not enough. They need the Bread o Life, too.

JACOB: (*looking down*) Yeah . . . and those guys building that combination gym, bowling alley, and movie theater . . . it's great they get to spend so much time together, but I hope they don't forget the most important thing they're supposed to be doing.

MIKE: (*pointing*) And then that group over there. (*shaking head*) . . . All the do is fight with each other.

JACOB: It's sad. They don't even see the <u>real</u> enemy.

MIKE: I know it. (*stands up, yelling "down" to the earth*) HELLO, CHRISTIAN! YOU'VE GOT A JOB TO DO! (*to JACOB*) You think they can hear us?

JACOB: I don't know, but it's worth a try. (*stands up, taking his turn*) THERE'S A LOT MORE ROOM UP HERE . . . GET BUSY! PLENTY OF MANSIONS TO GO AROUND.

MIKE: I guess we'll have to wait and see. One thing's for sure: They're the only ones who can do it.

(*after their last line, MIKE and JACOB walk off together as the lights fade and the music begins*)

"HEAVEN IS COUNTING ON YOU"

MARY/Mary
by Holly A. Baber

CAST
Mary-   a contemporary young mother (20s–early 30s)
MARY-   the mother of Jesus, in Biblical costume

SET/PROPS
A bare stage with a park bench (or chairs) is all that is required. Mary has a baby carrier or stroller with her.

(*Mary sits down on a bench and rests a baby carrier in front of her, so as not to be seen t the audience. Her bag is placed to the side. She looks up and down the road for her bus, and gently rocks the carrier with her foot.*)

(Seconds later, MARY, mother of Jesus, enters in her ancient clothes and hood, extremely pregnant, and eases onto the bench alongside Mary. MARY alternately holds her back and massages her stomach. She, too, is looking up and down the road.)

Mary: *(to her baby)* Where is it, sweetie? *(glancing at Mary)* Probably running late as usual.

MARY: Excuse me?

Mary: *(takes a good look at MARY for the first time)* We're talking about this bus and how it's late every year on December 24.

MARY: Is that today's date?

Mary: Yeah. Didn't you know that?

MARY: I am weary from all the travel. My husband and I have had a long journey.

Mary: We're lucky there's a bus taking us to my parents or we wouldn't be traveling at all. Right, Munchkin? *(smiles and coos at the baby)*

MARY: We rode around and around for hours before he would admit that we were lost. I never knew my Joseph possessed such stubbornness.

Mary: Well, men have been known to be like that.

MARY: I did not expect it from my husband.

Mary: Why wouldn't you?

MARY: We didn't know each other very long before we were married.

Mary: Oh. *(pauses for a couple of seconds, then her eyes grow wide with a different meaning)* Ohhhhh!

MARY: I didn't mean that . . .

Mary: *(laughing slightly)* It doesn't matter to me. My husband didn't exactly stick around for the baby. You're real lucky, you know?

(MARY grabs her back and winces at a sudden, sharp pain)

Mary: How close are your contractions?

MARY: Not very close. They just surprise me. Does it hurt much?

Mary: Yes, I'm afraid it does. (*looking around worried*) Where is your husband?

MARY: Getting our path straight.

Mary: Are you sure he didn't get lost getting directions? Men have been known to do that, too.

MARY: (*sitting upright again and looking amazingly serene*) He will be back shortly. We still have many miles to travel.

Mary: Where are you going?

MARY: Bethlehem.

Mary: Pennsylvania? I have cousins out that way. Do you know the Ronald Parkers?

MARY: No. (*closes her eyes and begins to hum very softly*)

Mary: Uhmmm . . . so, are you going home for the holidays?

MARY: We are going home to be counted.

Mary: I know exactly what you mean. I kind of felt that way, too, at my house. There are about a zillion cousins and we look just alike. I always got lost in the shuffle. But not now. Now with the baby, the crowds part like the Red Sea and I'm the Virgin Mary or something.

(*Mary and MARY now speak aloud to themselves, not hearing the other*)

MARY: (*MARY's eyes are closed again and she is rocking back and forth, breathing slowly*) I have traveled many moonless nights.

Mary: And even though nothing is like I planned when I was a little girl, now that I have this baby . . . it all makes sense. This is what I'm meant to do. It feels so right that sometimes it scares me.

MARY: Cold and weary with a babe inside and I wonder what I've done. You have come and chosen me now to carry Your Son.

Mary: You should see the looks on everyone's faces when we go home.

MARY: I am waiting in a silent prayer. (*eyes close*)

Mary: This little baby was like a tiny, ten-fingered light in the darkness.

MARY: (*opens her eyes and looks heavenward*) Do You wonder as You watch my face if a wiser one should have had my place?

Mary: Holding a baby is like holding the biggest piece of love you can imagine all wrapped up in your arms. Like a breath of heaven. (*looks to the right*) That's our bus. (*picks up the baby carrier and stands*) Next stop is Nana's house, Pumpkin. (*turns back to MARY*) I don't want to leave you here by yourself.

MARY: Joseph will be along shortly. Please. Go ahead. We are going to be just fine. It won't be much longer now. I can feel it.

Mary: That's what worries me.

MARY: We are safe in our Lord's hands.

Mary: (*leaves reluctantly*) Good luck to you.

MARY: You are a precious gift to your child. I wish you well in your journey.

Mary: Well, I hope your baby is as loved as mine is.

MARY: He will be.

Mary: It's a he? Congratulations. (*Mary exits stage right looking over her shoulder once at MARY and the glow that seems to hover over her.*)

(*music begins*)

MARY: But I offer all I am for the mercy of your plan. (*winces in another contraction*) Help me be strong.

"BREATH OF HEAVEN"

FIELD OF SOULS
A Musical
Script by Keith Ferguson

CHARACTERS

RANDY-   youth choir director, sincere, relaxed
SUSIE-   teenager, honest, curious, compassionate
MARK-   teenager, direct, out-going
JULIE-   typical teenager
DIANE-   Susie's friend since childhood, not a believer, cynical
JIM-   Mark's friend, new Christian

SETTING

The setting is a youth choir rehearsal, except for Scene 2, which takes place
outside of the high school, on a park bench.

SCENE 1

(*The setting is a youth choir rehearsal. The young people, dressed casually, enter the
scene making normal conversation among themselves. As the music begins for "Field of
Souls," everyone takes their places in singing positions. If desired, RANDY, the director
of the choir, can speak to the group first. For example: "Let's get started. We have a lot of
work to do today." At that point, the music could start.*)

"FIELD OF SOULS"

RANDY: Good job! Have a seat. That song is the main theme of our
            evangelism project that starts in two more weeks. If we're ever
            going to have an impact for Christ on our community, we're going
            to have to work together, right?

            (*The group just stares back at him. Some shift their weight awkwardly,
            look around, and are basically unresponsive. RANDY goes on anyway.*)

            Well, sure . . . of course we have to work together. Now, who can
            tell me what that last song is based on?

            (*Another awkward silence; general malaise. Just as RANDY is about to
            give up, we hear a voice.*)

SUSIE: Isn't it . . . sort of . . . like . . . from a Bible story?

RANDY: (*thrilled*) Yes! Not even sort of—it is from a Bible story. A specific
            kind of story. Does anybody know what kind?(*Again, silence.
            RANDY goes on slowly, drawing it out.*) A Par–a–

SUSIE: (*upbeat*) A parable?

RANDY: Yes! Good . . . great. All is not lost. And who taught parables?

MARK: Jesus.

RANDY: Alright! Now this parable is kind of unusual. Let me read it to you. Luke 8:5—(*reading from Bible*)
"A farmer went out to sow his seed. Some fell along the path; it was trampled on, and the birds of the air ate it up. Some fell on rock, and when it came up, the plants withered because they had no moisture. Other seeds fell among thorns, which grew up with it and choked the plants. Still other seed fell on good soil. It came up and yielded a crop, a hundred times more than was sown."

MARK: I don't get it.

RANDY: That's OK. Neither did the disciples. So Jesus explained it to them. "This is the meaning of the parable: The seed is the Word of God. Those along the path are the ones who hear, and then the devil comes and takes away the word from their hearts, so that they may not believe and be saved. Those on the rock are the ones who receive the word with joy when they hear it, but they have no root. They believe for a while, but after a time of testing, they fall away."

JULIE: (*interrupting*) Is that like . . . people who get saved at camp <u>every</u> year?

RANDY: (*careful*) Well . . . maybe . . . Let's keep going. Let's see . . . (*reads*) "The seed that fell among thorns stands for those who hear, but as they go on their way they are choked by life's worries, riches, and pleasures, and they do not mature."

SUSIE: That pretty much describes every male in the room, doesn't it?

    (*laughter, agreement, guys hiss, etc.*)

RANDY: OK, OK, here's the last one. (*reads*) "But the seed on good soil stands for those with a noble and good heart, who hear the word, retain it, and by persevering produce a crop." So, group. What does this say to us as we get ready to "evangelize?" (*stresses last word*)

SUSIE: I guess it means that everyone we witness to may not accept Christ.

RANDY: Right.

MARK: So that's when ya turn on the TV Preacher, huh? (*imitating evangelists*) HEY YOU—TURN OR BURN, BABY! GET RIGHT OR GET LEFT! GET ON GOD'S SIDE OR GET FRENCH FRIED!

RANDY: I don't think so, Mark.

SUSIE: (*to MARK*) As usual, you're a real turn-off. Randy, that's something that's always bothered me. I mean, what if people don't want Jesus? I don't want to feel like I'm acting like I'm better than them—like, well . . . "my God's better than your god . . . "

MARK: But He is!

RANDY: We have a responsibility to tell them the truth. Jesus said, "I am the Way, the Truth and the Life. No one comes to the Father except through Me." Jesus is not one of many ways—He is the only way to God. We can't waver on that. But, Susie, your question is very important. What we have to always remember, Mr. "Turn or Burn," is that love <u>has</u> to be the motivation behind evangelism. What's the one Scripture verse that almost everybody knows?

JULIE: John 3:16. "For God so loved the world that He gave His only beloved Son that whoever believes in Him will not perish, but will have everlasting life."

RANDY: Read the next verse.

JULIE: "For God did not send His Son into the world to condemn the world, but to save the world through Him."

SUSIE: So then . . . we shouldn't condemn either.

         (*music for "More Than Anything" begins*)

RANDY: Exactly. Evangelism in God's eyes is always about loving people . . . it's always about compassion for the individual. We need to have the heart of God.

"MORE THAN ANYTHING"

SCENE 2

(*After the song, the lights fade on the choir as SUSIE moves stage right and sits down on a chair, or park bench. She is either in her own light, or a follow spot. The lighting defines "another place," away from the choir. SUSIE is looking over a school project when her friend, DIANE, comes into the scene and sits down next to her.*)

DIANE: I thought I might find you out here. (*sits down next to SUSIE*)

SUSIE: Yeah, I thought I'd come out here and study before practice starts.

DIANE: So . . . anything exciting happen today?

SUSIE: Not much. Same old stuff. Brad was in sort of a bad mood.

DIANE: What about?

SUSIE: Who knows.

DIANE: Maybe he just needs some attention.

SUSIE: Don't tell him I said anything to you. Promise?

DIANE: Promise.

         (*on the "Promise" dialogue, they share some physical gesture that they've obviously done for years; a handshake, touching fingers, something that shows us that they've known each other for a long time*)

         He'll probably call you later.
         (*pause*) I saw you at lunch today. Why didn't you come on over and sit with us?

SUSIE: Well, . . . you guys seemed to be having a good time . . . I just don't feel comfortable . . .

DIANE: Sus, you know, those girls don't bite or anything. I know they're a little rowdy, they make a lot of noise and all that, but they're really OK.

SUSIE: I just don't fit in . . .

DIANE: No . . . maybe not.

SUSIE: Thanks a lot.

DIANE: You said it. I'm just agreeing with you.

SUSIE: I know, but this is the part where you're supposed to disagree with
            me and tell me that I do fit in and make me feel all better about the
            whole thing.

DIANE: That was junior high. This is high school. Now . . . we can be
            honest.

SUSIE: So . . . then, you're saying . . .

DIANE: Just that you need to let your hair down—live a little! I mean you
            are <u>always</u> so serious. You always do the right thing. Homework,
            guys, whatever—it doesn't matter. It gets old. I ask you to go do
            things and you always have a reason not to.

SUSIE: Diane, I've told you I'm not comfortable with all those people . . . or
            places.

DIANE: Nobody's going to make you do anything you don't want to do.
            I want to be with you, but, anymore, you just . . . aren't any fun.

SUSIE: Oh.

DIANE: Hey, don't get mad or anything. We've been friends since first
            grade. I love you, but . . . it's like . . . we just don't have the same
            relationship . . . something's different.

SUSIE: I know.

DIANE: You've noticed it, too?

SUSIE: Yeah. Diane, I don't know how to tell you what's different except
            that so many things have changed for me . . . inside.

DIANE: I don't understand.

SUSIE: It's God. I've become a Christian.

DIANE: *(not impressed)* So? I mean, hey—I believe in God. Does that mean we can't be friends?

SUSIE: No, not at all . . . it's just that . . .

DIANE: What? Are you too good for me now?

SUSIE: No. That's not what I'm saying.

DIANE: Then what . . .

SUSIE: My relationship with God is so . . . radical . . . that it's changed everything else in my life. It's changed every other relationship I have.

DIANE: No wonder Brad's freaking out. You're turning into . . . Mother Teresa . . . or something.

SUSIE: C'mon. You know that's not true. I wish I had the words to explain what I mean. I know you say you believe in God, but . . . do you know Him?

DIANE: As much as the next person, I guess. I'm not sure I know what you're talking about.

SUSIE: Alright, you said this was high school now, so we can be honest and all that.

DIANE: Right . . .

SUSIE: It's about knowing God in a personal way, through His Son, Jesus Christ.

DIANE: Or is it about knowing God <u>your</u> way.

SUSIE: I knew you would think that.

DIANE: OK—God, Jesus, Mohammed, Confucius, whoever . . . isn't it enough that I believe something?

SUSIE: Nobody else died for you, but Jesus.

DIANE: That's so dramatic.

SUSIE: But it's the truth. I know that if you knew how much God loves you . . . it would make a difference.

DIANE: (*pause*) I've got to go. Sorry if I made you mad or anything.

SUSIE: Don't worry about it. Diane, I know things have been a lot different between us lately, but, I really care about you . . . more than ever.

DIANE: I know you do. We'll talk some more.

SUSIE: Promise?

DIANE: Promise.

(*They exchange the same physical gesture as earlier on "Promise." DIANE leaves the stage as the music begins for "Dying to Reach You" begins. SUSIE could sing solo, if desired. The focus would shift back to the choir slowly, as they begin to sing, and the lights change.*)

"DYING TO REACH YOU"
SCENE 3

(*when the song ends, the group sits down in their places and SUSIE asks a question*)

SUSIE: Randy, what about the person who just doesn't seem to want God in their life—the person we just can't get through to?

RANDY: It's important to remember that it's not up to us to "get through to them." That is the Holy Spirit's job. He convicts their hearts that they need Jesus. What we can do is pray that God would draw them to Himself and that they would accept Christ.

SUSIE: But what can we say to them? What if we don't know the right words to say?

MARK: I think the best thing to tell someone is what God means to you—tell them what a difference Jesus has made in your own life.

JIM: Yeah, that's what Mark told me.

JULIE: What do you mean?

JIM: Mark is the first person who told me about Jesus.

JULIE: You don't mean it. <u>This</u> Mark?

JIM: Yep. Last year when my parents told me they were going to get divorced, I really got depressed . . . but I didn't tell anyone. I didn't want to talk about it. But I guess Mark noticed something was wrong. He asked me one day after baseball practice what was going on, so I told him.

MARK: I was just trying to be a friend. Anyway, I started talking to him about how God helped me through my parents' divorce. I told him I would have never made it through without Jesus. After about two weeks of talking to Jim, and praying for him, one day he just came up to me and said, "I want to be a Christian." So . . . we prayed right there in the outfield after practice.

JIM: It was really great. No big scene or nothing. No tears or big emotional high—just a real strong feeling that everything's OK—that I belong to God.

JULIE: Didn't you have a lot of questions?

JIM: Oh , sure. But, when I listened to Mark tell his story and talk about Jesus, I knew that I needed what he was talking about—I knew he was telling me the truth.

SUSIE: (*to MARK*) What did you say to him?

MARK: I just told him what a difference knowing Jesus made in my life. I told him the things I felt inside—in my heart. That's all I had to say, I guess.

(*music begins*)

"I WILL TELL THE WORLD"

SCENE 4

(*after song, the group relaxes into their sitting positions*)

RANDY: This has been a great rehearsal. We've talked through some important things. Now, in order to be ready for the FIELD OF SOULS project in two weeks, you need to identify that one person you are going to pray for and share Christ with. Even though we're going to talk to a lot of people as a group, you need to have that one person that you care about that you're going to trust God to reach. Remember what we talked about today. You're sharing Christ because of love—your love for God and your love for your friend.

SUSIE: But . . . what if they reject us? I'm still really worried about that.

RANDY: I know you are. But you have to remember that it is the Holy
           Spirit's job to draw them to Christ. You're not responsible for thei
           salvation. You're only responsible to be obedient to share—to be
           the light in the darkness. Here's what Jesus said after He shared tl
           parable of the sower with them.

           (opens Bible and reads)

           "No one lights a lamp and hides it in a jar or puts it under a bed.
           Instead, he puts it on a stand, so that those who come in can see tl
           light." Luke 8:16

           Let's go do it.

           "GO LIGHT YOUR WORLD"

SHINE ON US
A Worship Service for Choir & Readers
by Keith Ferguson

(The readings that precede each song should be delivered in an energetic, expressive style, not overly somber or "heavy." A "Reader's Theater" approach is recommended—readers can use black folders with their material inside, but should keep their face up and out to the audience, for maximum communication and facial expression. So, the material is presented as if memorized, in terms of confidence in presentation, even though the readers are using scripts.)

READER 1:   Shout for joy to the Lord, all the earth.

READER 2:   Worship the Lord with gladness;
Come before Him with joyful songs.

READER 3:   Know that the Lord is God. It is He who made us, and we are His.

READER 4:   We are His people, the sheep of His pasture.

READER 1:   Enter His gates with thanksgiving!

READER 2:   Enter His courts with praise!

READER 3:   Give thanks to Him and praise His name.

ALL: FOR THE LORD IS GOOD

READER 4:   And His love endures forever. His faithfulness continues through all generations. *(Psalm 100, NIV)*

READER 1:   We come together to worship God with thanksgiving,

READER 2:   Because of all that He has done for us.

READER 3:   We come to remember and proclaim His mighty acts of mercy and love.

READER 4:   In creation—

READER 1:   At Calvary—

READER 2:   And the resurrection.

READER 3:   And to praise and thank Him for meeting life's simplest and deepest needs.

READER 4:   He is the answer . . .

READER 1:   To life's ultimate questions.

READER 2:   We praise His name because He is worthy of praise.

READER 3:   Worship opens the door of intimacy with God, and reminds us of how much we need God's presence in our lives.

READER 4:   He is the Alpha and Omega, the beginning and the end. He create us and completes us.

READER 1:   He is Love!

READER 2:   He is Life!

READER 3:   He is Lord!

ALL: OVER EVERYTHING!

READER 4:   Join us as we celebrate Him together.

"HALLOWED BE THY NAME"

OPTIONS FOR CONGREGATIONAL SINGING:
The Hymnal for Worship & Celebration, Word Music, © 1986
#96 or #97 "All Hail the Power of Jesus' Name"
#99 - #103 "The Name of Jesus"—Medley

Songs for Praise & Worship, Word Music, © 1992
#79   "No Other Name"
#80   "Blessed Be the Name of the Lord"
#87   "Praise the Name of Jesus"
#88   "His Name Is Life"
#100 "Bless the Name of Jesus"

READER 1:   The Psalmist proclaimed that "in His presence, there is fullness of joy."

READER 2:   We find pleasure and peace in celebrating God's goodness together.

READER 3:   There should be excitement and energy in our worship.

READER 4:   And yet, joy and celebration are only a part of a true worship experience. Confession and repentance are also important elements of encountering God in worship.

READER 1:   Too often, we overlook these important requirements for experiencing genuine worship, but we cannot escape the need for them.

READER 2:   The prophet Isaiah had a worship experience that can serve as a model for experiencing God.

READER 3:   In the year that King Uzziah died, I saw the Lord seated on a throne, high and exalted, and the train of His robe filled the temple.

READER 4:   Above Him were seraphs, each with six wings: With two they covered their faces, with two they covered their feet, and with two they were flying. And they were calling to one another:

ALL: "HOLY, HOLY, HOLY IS THE LORD ALMIGHTY;
THE WHOLE EARTH IS FULL OF HIS GLORY."

READER 1:   At the sound of their voices the doorposts and thresholds shook and the temple was filled with smoke.

READER 2: "Woe to me!" I cried. "I am ruined! For I am a man of unclean lips, and I live among a people of unclean lips, and my eyes have seen the King, the Lord Almighty."

READER 3: Then one of the seraphs flew to me with a live coal in his hand, which he had taken with tongs from the altar. With it he touched my mouth and said,

READER 4: "See, this has touched your lips: your guilt is taken away and your sin atoned for."

READER 1: Then I heard the voice of the Lord saying,

READER 2: "Whom shall I send? And who will go for us?"

READER 1: And I said,

ALL: "HERE AM I. SEND ME!" (*from Isaiah 6:1–8*)

(*pause*)

READER 3: O God, as we worship You, may we be so awed by Your holiness,

READER 4: So convicted by Your righteousness,

READER 1: That we are moved to confession . . .

READER 2: . . . repentance

READER 3: . . . and obedience.

READER 4: Hear the voice of the Lord— "Be ye holy, as I am holy."

"YOU ARE HOLY"

OPTIONS FOR CONGREGATIONAL SINGING:
The Hymnal for Worship & Celebration, Word Music, © 1986
#262 "Holy, Holy, Holy"
#266 "Holy, Holy"
#437 "Pure and Holy"

Songs for Praise & Worship, Word Music, © 1992
#34 "Come into the Holy of Holies"
#37 "Holy, Holy, Holy (Hosanna)"
#71 "When I Look into Your Holiness"

READER 1: Let us pause to reflect on the holiness, beauty, and grace of our Lord. Take this time to pray quietly where you are, asking God to reveal Himself and His will to you in these moments.

(pause—silence or appropriate instrumental music here)

READER 2: O Lord, hear our prayer. We want to be different because of this experience. Help us to be open to Your Spirit, to have yielded hearts toward You . . .

READER 3: We confess that often we come to worship unprepared and unwilling to be truly changed.

READER 4: Yet, we long to be <u>transformed</u> by Your presence. We are needy. We are dependent on You, O God. We need Your grace . . .

READER 1: We need Your love . . .

READER 2: Your peace . . .

READER 3: Your light . . .

READER 4: Your life . . .

"SHINE ON US"

READER 1: Worship is really a response . . .

READER 2: . . . a response to the love that God has shown us, in Christ.

READER 3: Thus, true worship must be Christ-centered.

READER 4: For every time we gather, we remember God's love expressed through His Son.

READER 1: We remember the cross, the sacrifice for our sin, and the forgiveness we have been given in Christ.

READER 2: And we commit to living a "crucified life" of self-denial—dying to ourselves . . .

READER 3: But living the life of the Resurrection! For Jesus Christ rose again! We have His resurrection life available to us! Because of the resurrection, we can have an intimate love relationship with God.

READER 4: God is the initiator of this love relationship—He came to us, and this great love demands a response.

READER 1: "This is how we know what love is: Jesus Christ laid down His life for us."

READER 2: "This is how God showed His love among us: He sent His one and only Son into the world that we might live through Him.

READER 3: This is love: not that we loved God, but that He loved us and sent His Son as an atoning sacrifice for our sins.

READER 4: If anyone acknowledges that Jesus is the Son of God, God lives in him, and he in God.

ALL: AND SO WE KNOW AND RELY ON THE LOVE GOD HAS FOR US." (*1 John 3:16, 9–10, 15–16*)

"THE LOVE OF CHRIST"

(At this point, the pastor or minister could offer an invitation to spiritual decision, i.e., accepting Christ as Savior, in recognition of God's great love, or recommitting to a love relationship with God through worship, prayer and Bible study. Communion is also a strong option at this point.)

OPTIONS FOR CONGREGATIONAL SINGING:
The Hymnal for Worship & Celebration, Word Music, © 1986
#512 "My Savior's Love"
#513 "Oh, How He Loves You and Me"

Songs for Praise & Worship, Word Music, © 1992
#112 "Lamb of God"
#114 "I'm Forever Grateful"
#220 "You Are My All in All"